CONNECTED
FOR
GOD'S
PURPOSE

A DEVOTIONAL COLLECTION OF STORIES

BY DAUGHTERS OF THE KING

Published in the United States of America
Publisher: Luminous Publishing
www.luminouspublishing.com
For bulk orders or other inquiries, email:
info@luminouspublishing.com

TABLE OF CONTENTS

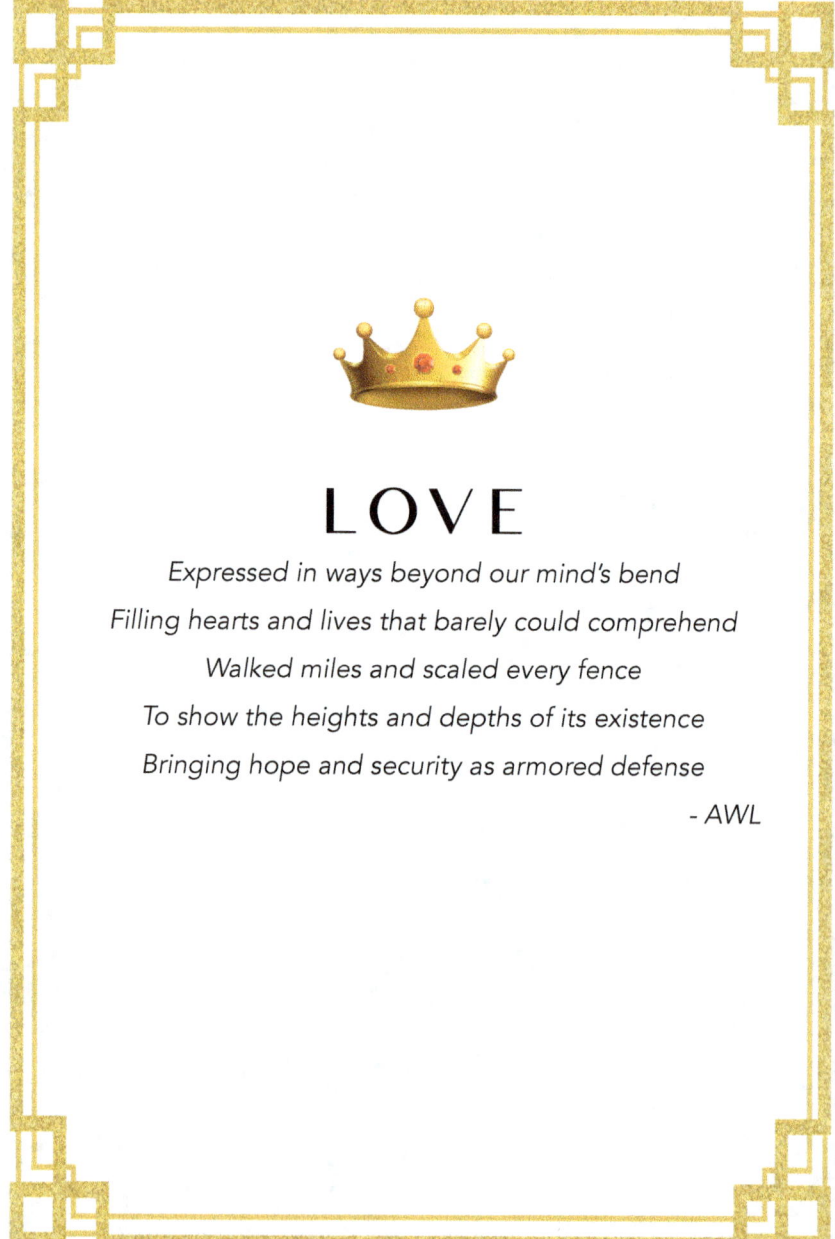

LOVE

Expressed in ways beyond our mind's bend
Filling hearts and lives that barely could comprehend
Walked miles and scaled every fence
To show the heights and depths of its existence
Bringing hope and security as armored defense

- AWL

Abide in Me

~ Shanae Clarke ~

"Abide in me, and I in you. As the branch cannot bear fruit of itself, except it abide in the vine; no more can ye, except ye abide in me."
- John 15:4, (KJV)

Christianity is not about performing rituals or checking off a to-do list - it's about relationship. The word abide is synonymous with the word remain; in most Bible translations, the phrase is often interchangeable. Jesus made it a priority to remain anchored to the Father – He would spend early mornings and late hours into the night in fellowship with God. He didn't lean on His own understanding when it came to selecting the disciples, choosing to go to Samaria, or determining in His heart to go to the Cross in the Garden of Gethsemane. He trusted in God through it all, and we, as His disciples, are called to the same.

In John 15, Jesus describes Himself as the True Vine, God the Father as the gardener, and His disciples as the branches. As the gardener, the Father is responsible for pruning the branches so they can bear more fruit; -which is symbolic of the sanctification process for the life of the believer. And through our yielding to Christ, the Holy Spirit causes fruit to be produced in our lives. Jesus' use of this metaphor illustrates that without our connection to Him, we can do nothing, and He is the sole Sustainer. A branch that is cut off from the vine cannot produce fruit nor sustain the ones it has - rather, it withers and eventually dies. In Acts 17: 28, Paul further solidifies this relationship when he writes, "For in him we live and move, and have our being…"

You have to choose to abide in Christ and to be anchored to Him. We can easily fall prey to working within our own strength while walking in our purpose in a culture that preaches autonomy. And in doing so, we become like that branch that is dry and delusional and eventually seduced by other doctrines.

Total dependence on Christ and on the finished work at Calvary is the only way to produce fruit that will remain. It is the only way for the fruits and gifts of the Spirit to be manifested in our lives that will transform nations. It is the only way that, even in the midst of persecution and trials, we will run the race that is set before us.

PRAYER

Dear God,

Help me to remain connected to You and renew my mind to under-stand that You are the Source of my Strength. My relationship with You is not based on what I can do for You but on what You want to do with me and through me. I choose to go through the refining process so that I will produce fruit that will remain. Amen

Are you Martha?

~ Shanae Clarke ~

"Martha, Martha," the Lord answered, "you are worried and upset about many things, but few things are needed—or indeed only one. Mary has chosen what is better, and it will not be taken away from her." - Luke 10:41-42, NIV

One Sunday, as I was heading to work, I heard that still small voice ask, "Are you, Martha?" I replied, "No, I am Shanae." He asked two more times, and I still answered, saying Shanae. Baffled that He was confusing me with someone else, I shrugged off His comment. A couple of nights later, I was still perplexed about the question, and I asked the Holy Spirit to clarify the matter at hand. He revealed it to me in a Daily Word devotional entitled, "Are you too busy?"

In verse 38 of Luke 10, we find Jesus visiting the house of Martha and her sister Mary. Upon His arrival, Mary was mesmerized by Jesus and was sitting at His feet, listening to Him. Martha, however, was busy in the kitchen and was upset when she saw Mary just sitting there. Martha was frustrated and asked Jesus to reprimand her for not helping. After all, she needed help in the kitchen. A guest was at their house, and not just any guest. It was Jesus! I mean, who wouldn't be in the kitchen anxiously preparing food for Him. Instead of talking to Mary, Jesus says, "Martha, Martha, (He calls her name twice to get her attention) you are worried and upset about many things. But (one thing is needed), and Mary has chosen what is better, and it will not be taken away from her."

As I read the story, and trust me, I read it more than once, the Holy Spirit began to work on my heart and revealed that, like Martha, I was busy doing what I thought were good things. I was busy focusing on school, my career, — you know, things that would help me make a name for myself. But in the process of doing that, I wasn't actively pursuing and prioritizing God in my life. I wasn't taking the time to know and cultivate a relationship with Him. And that is what Mary realized at that moment when Jesus walked into her sister's house.

She saw an opportunity not to get up and serve Him with food, but she saw a chance to receive from the giver of life. I mean, this is the same Jesus that told the lady at the well, "...whoever drinks the water that I give will never thirst..." (John 4:14, NIV)

Upon receiving this revelation, my life has been transformed for the better as the Lord reaffirms to me every day that I can do nothing without Him and that everything I need is in Him. Good works cannot get me into heaven, but rather a covenant relationship and a repentant heart will. I know that many of us on the Day of Judgment want to hear Jesus say, "Well done, good and faithful servant ... Come and share your master's happiness!" (Matthew 25:23, NIV). But the Bible states that some will hear, even though they did many great things in the Lord's name. "'I never knew you. Away from me" (Matthew 7:23, NIV).

Today I challenge those reading this testimony to take a page from the life of Mary and choose what Jesus describes as that one needful thing. The Bible says the only way to get to the Father is through His Son, Jesus Christ, so make a decision and choose this day whom you will serve. If you are not sure, ask the Holy Spirit, who is the revealer of all truth, to lead you into a covenant relationship with Jesus.

PRAYER

Dear God,
Forgive me for building up my own dreams and living my life
without a relationship with You. You are the potter, and I am the clay
- I am the work of Your hands, so I surrender my life completely to
You. Please help me to put You first in everything I do. Holy Spirit, I
give You permission to remove every idol in my heart and the
distractions of this world that keep me separated from You,
in Jesus' name. Amen.

Loving You to Death

~ Tecora Noble ~

"Greater love has no one than this, than to lay down one's life for his friends." - John 15:13, NKJV

Have you ever sat and really contemplated John 3:16?

"For God so loved the world (you and I) that He gave his only be-gotten Son, that whosoever believeth in him should not perish but have everlasting life." - John 3:16, KJV

Wow, what a powerful and amazing love statement. Consider also John 15:13 (NKJV), which states, "Greater love has no man than this, than to lay down one's life for his friends." When we realize and recognize the love our Heavenly Father and Savior have for us, we can confidently say, "my God really loves me to death. He gave His life for me so that I can have life and live more abundantly." Jesus took all our pains and bore our sufferings. He was wounded for our transgressions; He was bruised for our —and not His — iniquities. He who knew no sin but became our sin (2 Corinthians 5:21 (NIV). What a mighty God we serve.

Have you ever wondered or even said, "Wow, God gave up His only Son for me!" or "Jesus gave His life for me?" This is what you call loving someone to death, and that someone is me and also you. You are eternally loved by God. Romans 8:35 (CEV) asks, "Can anything separate us from the love of Christ? Can trouble, suffering, and hard times, hunger and nakedness, or danger and death? What shall we then say to these things? If God be for us, who can be against us?" Again, we are challenged to observe His great love in verse 32 of the same chapter, where it states, "He that spared not His own Son, but delivered Him up for us all, how shall He not with Him also freely give us all things?"

Not only did He give up His only Son to die for us, but He has promised to freely provide for us! In other words, God, in all His awesomeness and love, will do anything for us! Isn't God's love unmatchable? Absolutely, no one can ever fathom it!

As a youth in Sunday School, I remember singing many wonderful songs, but the one I loved the most was "Jesus Loves Me This I Know for the Bible Tells Me So." I loved this song because I felt loved by God even though I truly didn't know much about Him. All I knew was that He loved me, and I could go into the Bible to be reminded of His love. I never truly understood the importance of these words and God's unconditional love until I got older and created an intimate relationship with Him. His Spirit helped me to truly understand the value of God's love, and now I can say not only the Bible tells me so because I've personally experienced God's love for myself. My pastor calls it an "in-to-me-I see" relationship. It's also stated, "That the greatest knowledge is to know the love of Jesus." I am happy I have received this knowledge, and it is available to everyone for free. Jesus' love endures forever and ever and spreads to all generations. His love is infinite and never failing. With this act of love, be encouraged to seek refuge in the fact that nothing, and I mean nothing...absolutely nothing, or anyone, can separate you from God's love.

PRAYER

Abba Father, who art in heaven, hallowed be Your name. Thank You, God, for loving me to death and beyond it. Your love is everlasting, without end. Thank You for giving me Your Son to save my life so I can live freely in and with You. Lord, forgive me if I ever doubted Your love towards me or even forgot Your promise that nothing can ever separate me from Your love. Help me to realize Your steadfast love endures forever. In Jesus' name. Amen

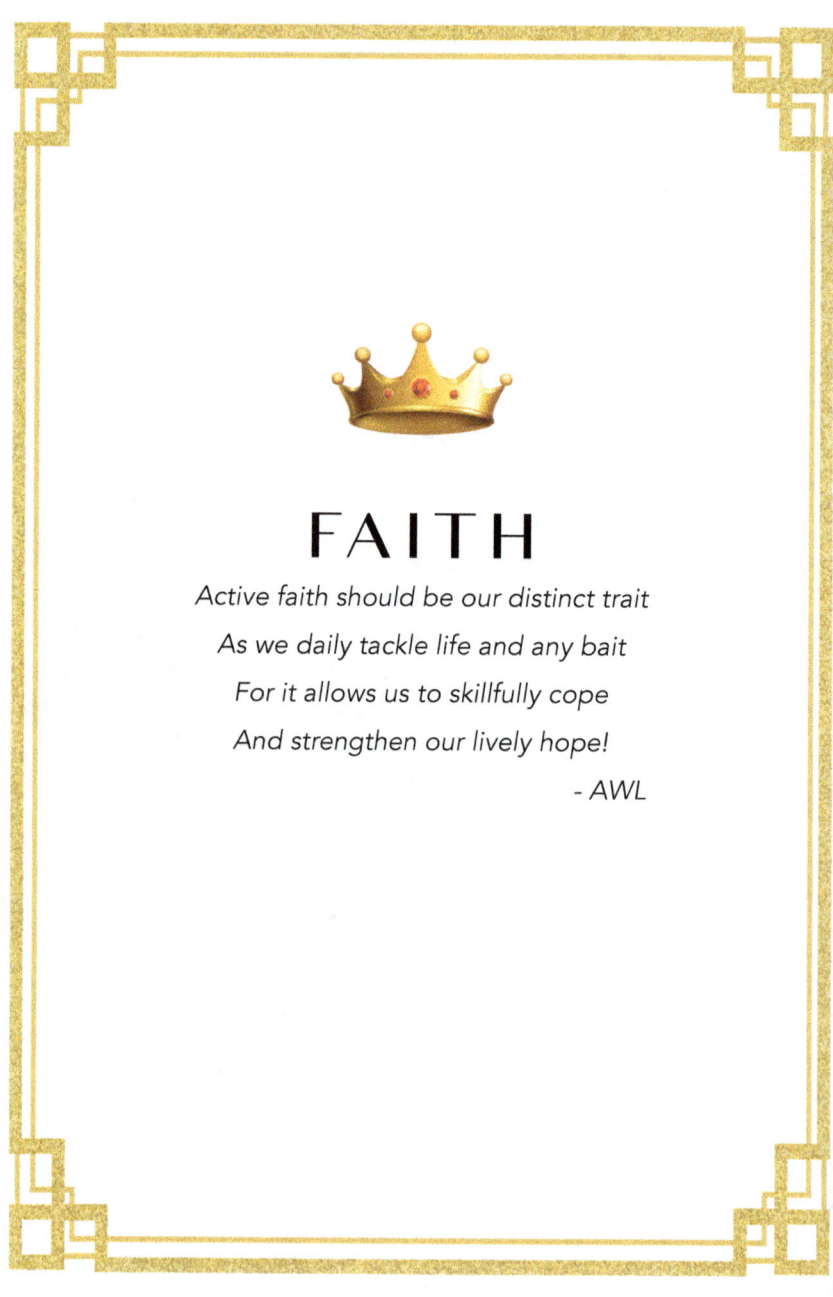

FAITH

Active faith should be our distinct trait

As we daily tackle life and any bait

For it allows us to skillfully cope

And strengthen our lively hope!

- AWL

What's Blocking Your Vision

~ Petrice Dyer ~

"For we walk by faith and not by sight."
- 2 Corinthians 5:7, KJV

On my way to work, as I drove on the freeway, the sun was rising in the direction I was heading. The sun was right in my line of vision. Unfortunately, I could not see clearly. I quickly adjusted my visor to block out the rays of the sun. Then this question dropped into my thoughts: "In your Christian journey, can you see where you're going? Is there anything preventing you from getting to that place where God wants you to be? What is hindering you from reaching the mark, that higher calling in Jesus?

As you travel this pilgrim journey (through life), sometimes you will come to a point where your vision is obscured. Keep going, and adjust your visor (FAITH) to help you maneuver the journey. The Bible reminds us in 2 Corinthians 5:7 that we walk by faith and not by sight. No matter how dark the road ahead may seem, trust God even when you cannot see. Don't turn back, don't detour, stay the course. Don't abort the journey.

Faith can help you override any obstacle that may prevent you from achieving God's best. So, put on your spiritual glasses. Accept the path God is leading you down. Do not fear what lies ahead.

PRAYER

Lord, give me the vision to see things like You do. Release anything paralyzing my God-given purpose--old habits, past hurts, pain, pride, negativity. Rid me of anything that is obscuring my vision of getting to You. Help me to see You in every area of my life. Help me not to stumble and give in to temptation in Jesus' name. Amen.

"For we Walk by Faith, Not by Sight"

~ Tecora Noble ~

"For we walk by faith, not by sight."
- 2 Corinthians 5:7, KJV

This familiar scripture is known by all Christians -- one that's mostly reiterated in every believer's life. But I truly wonder if we comprehend this scripture and how it can and will change our thinking and life. The Holy Spirit awaken my spirit to understand this, so I may edify you, my sisters. When you carefully study and digest 2 Corinthians 5:7, you may realize it does not state that we are to walk with faith, nor does it state that we are to walk with sight. It states we walk by faith, not by sight. I truly believe most Christians are walking with faith and not by faith. What do I mean?

When I look at the definition of "by," it states identifying the agent performing an action, which points to faith (the agent) in action. Then I looked at the definition of "with," it states, "possessing (something) as a feature or accompaniment. If we walk with faith, we are leading and allowing faith to follow, wrong! Let me explain.

Have you ever gone somewhere and invited someone "with" you. That person is a guest, the tag-along, and at times may feel uncomfortable. We should not let faith be just an escort but the primary source of all we do. We need to let faith be the agent initiating our actions, so we can see the hand of God moving and bringing forth greatness in our lives.

Faith needs movements. As Steve Harvey stated, "we will have to leap." So, leap and let God be the parachute, aligning us into doors and opportunities.

When the scripture tells us faith without works is dead, it truly means faith is dead without action. Faith is useless without action. Faith cannot move unless you move. Faith cannot do what it was sent here to do if you don't ACT. Are you hearing me, sisters? Faith is not a crutch we should use to live the Christian life or to help us feel better by saying, "God will provide."

We don't walk by sight because sight is the ability to see images up close and far away. Vision goes beyond what the eye can see and further. Because faith is aligned with vision, it already sees what the eyes do not; it is the evidence of things not seen. I think that's what we've been doing all these years, walking with faith — which is not bad, but it doesn't manifest anything because we are doing it by our own ability. Faith is the transportation to our destination. We envision where we want to go; we see where we want to be; we visualize who we want to become. But when we start, faith makes all things work together for our good. If we are saying, God will provide, then, sister, show me your sacrifice. If none, it means you are just waiting for faith to manifest, and that is a lost hope.

By faith, Abel acted. By faith, Noah acted. By faith, Abraham acted. By faith, we should act. So, put God in your faith mobile. Remember, it's not by your strength, nor your own ability, but only through and by the Spirit of God.

PRAYER

Abba Father, who art in heaven, thank You for allowing me from this day forward to walk by faith and not by sight. Help me not to be discouraged but to act knowing for certain that all things will work together for my good. As I step out in faith, empower me to stay under Your grace and help others to accept You and walk by faith, too. Amen.

PATIENCE

Great wait is what most of us deem as weight

But God expects us to do it without debate

For though we cannot fathom the reason,

We must, in stillness, try not to grow weary in this season.

He may not reveal to us all the details

But if we trust His leading, this period of waiting,

Can be done without fighting and screaming.

So stop trying to analyze everything

Allow Him to do all the thinking and instructing

And though you feel, like in it all, you are drowning

Just believe Him for the final crowning!

- AWL

God's No!

~ Petrice Dyer ~

"Wait for the Lord; be strong and take heart and wait for the Lord."
- Psalm 27:14, NIV

When God says no, can you still trust Him?

The answer is yes, you can. When we pray, we are in a place of expectancy. We await answers from God in our favor. When we pray, we ask God for good things like healing during sickness and money when we are broke, but sometimes the things we desire don't get fulfilled — at least not when we want them to. In Philippians 4:6, we are told, "Be careful for nothing but in everything with prayer and supplication and with thanksgiving make your request known unto God."(KJV). We may never comprehend why our requests are not answered immediately, but we have to trust His will for our life.

God will never withhold any good thing from us. He will fulfill that which He promises in His own time, wisdom, and purpose. Our answer may be delayed, but it doesn't mean it's denied. Asking and receiving an unfavorable response can be tough. In Isaiah 40:31, we are reminded that "... they that wait upon the Lord, shall renew their strength, they shall mount up with wings as eagles, they shall run and not be weary; and they shall walk and not faint." (KJV)

Today, I want you to "trust the process and wait patiently on God." Sometimes He has to close some chapters in our lives to protect us. Don't try to help God in the process. He's God all by Himself. The All-sufficient One, God Almighty is He!

PRAYER

Lord, thank You for all my answered prayers, both yes and no. Help me to understand Your will for my life. Help me to trust Your "no." Give me grace and strength to make it through Your "no." No matter the answer or outcome, I believe with You, all things are possible. Grant me wisdom to pray and wait upon You always.
In Jesus' name. Amen.

"Wait on the Lord"

~ Patrice Reid ~

*"Wait on the LORD: be of good courage, and he shall
strengthen thine heart: wait, I say, on the LORD."
- Psalms 27:14, KJV*

We sing it, preach it, pray about it, and even journal our times with Him. Yet, it is not until we are faced with a situation that seems impossible, and have no other choice, that we truly experience what it means to wait on the Lord. Yes, it is then that we truly know what it means to "be of good courage and He will strengthen your heart."

I have been through several seasons of waiting, and I am still in awe as to how I made it through. I spent time praying, fasting, and studying things to advance me academically and spiritually while serving in ministry. I remember for weeks, I felt like I was in labor-like pain and constantly had to pray through it. I would call almost every Intercessor I knew to agree with me in prayer, and I remember telling somebody I felt like God was killing me, and as clear as day, she said in her Jamaican patois, "Yu no start dead yet," which is interpreted as (you haven't started dying yet). And after every episode, I had a new idea or missional duty assignment to complete and many financial or relational breakthroughs. I was always like I went through all that for this moment. The season became smoother yet still challenging there on.

I felt so pregnant with great possibilities during almost every season. Every season it was like the old me (that old wineskin) was dying. A more refined me (the new wine) was coming forth with such force that the people around me could not understand me. During those times, I wasn't even sure what was happening to me. There were some very lonely times, but the truth of God's Word strengthened me and made me strong.

There were seasons I questioned the Father about things He had revealed to me, which were still waiting to manifest. I can remember asking, "Lord, how is it that this and that person were doing this, and saying that, and I have to stay in prayer and fasting constantly? When will it be my turn?" I would always hear "wait" or "not yet time." At one time, I even heard, "what we have is not for show." I was reminded of Hannah as she waited in grief for a child to the point where her husband asked her, "Am I not better to thee than ten sons?" (1 Samuel 1:8, KJV). When God reminds me of this, it always melts my heart and gets me back into the waiting line and posture.

Today, I hope you will be courageous and strengthened every mile of the way as you choose to endure this time and wait on the Lord.

PRAYER

Lord, I thank You for this season of waiting. I pray the life of each person who reads this today will be transformed as they go through their waiting season. I pray the truth of Your Word will sustain them as they wait upon You, in Jesus' name. Amen.

While we Wait on God

~ Petrice Dyer ~

"But they that wait upon the Lord shall renew their strength; they shall mount up with wings as eagles; they shall run, and not be weary; and they shall walk, and not faint." - Isaiah 40:31, KJV

Do you ever feel exhausted waiting for something to happen? Waiting can be painful, but it should not be a place of frustration. While we wait for God to answer our prayers, God is waiting on us to elevate our faith, trust Him, and give Him praise while we wait. Of course, our human nature will cause us to fast-track the process, but we ought to exercise patience and trust God's will for our lives.

We must understand that the script is already written. God doesn't need our assistance. He needs our total dependence on Him. No matter the plans we put in place, our lives will only actualize according to God's will and purpose. Do not lose hope; there is a reward in the wait.

God's words in Isaiah 40:31 reminds us that He is desirous of advancing us if we wait patiently on Him. He wants us to mount up with wings as eagles. All we have to do is trust His divine timing for our lives.

Sometimes God has a beautiful gift waiting for us, but we settle for second best because we get so apprehensive and impatient. Philippians 4:6-7 reminds us not to be anxious for anything, but when we pray (make our request known), we should be thankful and remain tolerant for God to grant us the desires of our hearts.

PRAYER

Father in heaven, we bow down to Your will and to Your way. Help us to understand that when we pray, it's according to Your will and not ours. Help us run the race with patience, knowing that You are the author and finisher of our faith. Help us not to get weary in well-doing. Lord, help us to trust the process and learn the lessons as You prepare us for abundance. In our weakness, may You give us strength. Help us to wait patiently on You. We surrender all our cares. We trade all our sorrows for Your joy, in Jesus' name. Amen.

ABANDON

Walk away - step out of that place or character,
you know should not be named among you.

AVOIDANCE IS NOT ENOUGH!

Instead, engage in grave action, so you can advance
in the kingdom.

Hastily flee and refrain from any form of regret

For these your appetite should not whet

Forward steps of strength with courage like a lion

And your Father's keen wisdom is what you should rely on

If you are to conquer any trace of these devious dark
matters and return from oblivion.

ABANDON, ABANDON
& WILLFULLY PRESS ON.

- AWL

Fear is a Spirit – Cast it Out!

~ Shauna-Kay Calder ~

"For the Spirit God gave us does not make us timid, but gives us power, love, and self-discipline."
- 2 Timothy 1:7, NIV

God speaks to us — His people — as our Creator. God has a special and unique claim upon us because He is our Creator. Knowing we belong to the Lord is a wonderful answer to fear. We know that He holds us, protects us, guards us, and cares for us. We know He would not have created, redeemed, and called us unless He intended to finish His work in us.

How can we be afraid when we know this God is for us and looking out for our interests? "For God has not given us a spirit of fear but of power and of love and of a sound mind." Paul wrote this to Timothy because boldness matters. Without it, we can't fulfill God's purpose for our lives. God's purpose for us is more than making money, being entertained, and being comfortable. It is for each of us to use the gifts He gave us to touch His people and help a needy world.

Unfortunately, we all face situations where we feel timid and afraid. For some, speaking in front of others makes them afraid. Others are afraid of confrontation, some are scared of looking foolish, and others are afraid of rejection. We all deal with fear. Fear is a spirit that puts people in bondage and torment (Romans 8:15, KJV).

The first step in dealing with such fears is to understand that they are not from God. It is a significant step to say, "This isn't God making me feel like this; God hasn't given me this." Perhaps it is from personality, perhaps a weakness of the flesh, perhaps a demonic attack, but it isn't from God. We don't need to accept what God has not given us — a spirit of fear. The clear emphasis is "do not fear." What we need to do is humbly receive and walk in what He has given us, a spirit of power, love, and of a sound mind.

33

Fear and timidity will keep us from using the gifts God gives. God wants each of us to take His power, His love, and His calm thinking, to overcome fear, and to be used by Him with all the gifts He gives. He that fears God needs to fear no one else.

PRAYER

Dear Lord, in Isaiah 41:10, You reminded me, "Don't be afraid, for I am with you. Don't be discouraged, for I am your God. I will strengthen you and help you. I will hold you up with my victorious right hand." You know that we live in a crazy and chaotic world. You also know my struggles in my daily life. Please reduce the feelings of fear and anxiety that plague me. Calm me, and open my heart to Your peace and wisdom. As I seek to replace negative fear with good fear and strive to live in a way that respects You, help me rest in You, and trust You as I navigate this life, in Jesus' name. Amen.

A Jealous Heart

~ Lacyann Nation ~

"But when his brothers saw that their father loved him more than all his brothers, they hated him and could not speak peacefully to him."
- Genesis 37:4, NKJV

At some point or another, we have all felt some level of envy towards another person. The important thing is that we recognize this behavior and work to change it before it gets worse. If not, it will consume you and cause you to do something you never thought imaginable of yourself. Be honest with yourself, even at this moment, and ask yourself:

What does someone have that you feel that you should have, too?
Do you think you deserve it more than they do?
Why do you feel this way?

Joseph's brothers were faced with envy, and they continued to embrace it until they reached the point where they conspired to kill Joseph. However, they did end up selling him instead. All this was because his brothers were jealous of him being favored by his father. He then had a beautiful multicolored robe made for him by his father. I imagine this only fueled the envy that they already had towards Joseph. Joseph told them of his dreams that showed they would bow down to him, which further added to the raging jealousy already brewing inside them. It only pushed them over the edge and made them so consumed by envy that they were no longer thinking or acting logically. He became a problem that they needed to get rid of to feel better about themselves.

The brothers did not at any point try to recognize the darkness growing inside their hearts and make a change. In order to fix a problem, you first have to acknowledge that there is a problem. God loves us, and He doesn't want us to be jealous of each other. He has blessed us all in different ways with what He knows we genuinely need. We

need to be happy for each other. We need to encourage each other. We need to support each other. Sometimes we get our blessings
through inspiring and helping others. Don't let jealousy consume you.
A jealous heart is not a happy heart.

PRAYER

Dear God, I have seen in me a jealous heart, but I want to be happy and supportive of others. Cleanse my heart of all envious feelings and my mind of all jealous thoughts. Help me to be content with what You have blessed me with.
In Jesus' name. Amen.

ARISE

Be fierce and fearless

As you step out to achieve your best

Look not on each test

Confidently glide, quelling every Notion

of disguise

Focus your attention on the prize

As you from negations powerfully arise.

- AWL

Come Out of Hiding

~ Shanae Clarke ~

"The Spirit of the Lord GOD is upon me; because the LORD hath anointed me to preach good tidings unto the meek; he hath sent me to bind up the brokenhearted, to proclaim liberty to the captives, and the opening of the prison to them that are bound; 2 To proclaim the acceptable year of the LORD, and the day of vengeance of our God; to comfort all that mourn."
- Isaiah 61:1-2, KJV

By avoiding childhood trauma, we can create wounds that reappear in our adult lives. They can resurface and affect us emotionally, spiritually, and physically. Many of us seek help through counseling, but even therapists have found this hypothesis to be true. For instance, prior to addressing issues that a patient is currently facing, they would often ask questions about their past to find a correlation between the past and the present.

A song written by Steffany Gretzinger called "Out of Hiding" reflects Jesus' heart for the broken. The song depicts an invitation to us to come out from the shadows of our trauma to receive the redemption that His sacrifice paid for us. The emphasis of Jesus' sacrifice for our sins is widely preached today, and that's really great, but I think we do people a disservice when we don't preach the total victory received for even those wounds hidden behind the seams of our hearts.

After Jesus' forty days in the wilderness, He goes to Nazareth and makes this proclamation at the start of His ministry. Today we can compare this to a President/Prime Minister giving an inaugural speech to start their term. Jesus actually reiterated the words found in the book of Isaiah, "The Spirit of the Lord is upon me because He hath anointed me to preach the Gospel to the poor; He hath sent me to heal the brokenhearted, to preach deliverance to the captives, and recovering of sight to the blind, to set at liberty them that are bruised. To preach the acceptable year of the Lord" (Luke 4:18-19, KJV). It's important to keep in mind that Jesus was focused on transformation.

This proof is displayed all throughout the gospels by the first-hand account of His disciples. These men witnessed Him healing the sick, delivering the oppressed, and restoring those bound in a lifestyle of sin.

Moreover, the God we serve does not get weary or tired of us, and He is not intimidated by our past (Isaiah 40:28, KJV). We don't have to hide it, and we don't have to run away from Him. No matter the trauma or issue at hand, I pray today that you will take part in God's Grand Exchange. May you receive "beauty for ashes, the oil of joy for mourning, and the garment of praise for the spirit of heaviness" (Isaiah 61:3, KJV). With Christ as our mediator, we have the opportunity to come close to the Father again. The stigma of our past does not have any hold over us when we give them to Jesus and allow Him to heal the wounds (especially the dark hidden ones).

PRAYER

Dear God, I am tired of running and hiding in the shadows of my circumstances. I realize now that I can't save myself. I don't want to cover up my issues anymore. All my deep, dark secrets and wounds are Yours. I want to be free from them. I want to be whole. Right now, I give You access into every area of my life; please, heal the trauma of my past so that I can walk in total freedom. Your Word is spirit, and it is life - so I ask that You sanctify me through and through. Help me to forgive those that have hurt me and to declare Your Word as my true identity, in Jesus' name. Amen.

"Bent but not Broken"

~ Petrice Dyer ~

*"And a woman was there who had been crippled by a spirit for eigh-
teen years. She was bent over and could not straighten up at all.
When Jesus saw her, he called her forward and said to her, "Woman,
you are set free from your infirmity." Then he put his hands on her,
and immediately she straightened up and praised God."*
- Luke 13:11-13, NIV

Perhaps the journey that you have been on has been tiring and
exhausting. Though it may be, did you know that the burden of it
all doesn't belong to you; the victory does. Your success is not determined by time. It's your ability to endure irrespective of what life
throws at you. "Blessed is the man that endures temptation: for when
he is tried, he shall receive the crown of life, which the Lord hath
promised to them that love him" (James 1:12, KJV). It's having the
willpower and the faith to not give in to the temptations of life.

When you are bowed down, keep pushing your way through.
Realize that even though you are bent, you're not broken. Your situation is not permanent, but your victory is. You may be cast down,
feel rejected, and crippled in your situation, but remember that in
your waiting, God is working. Don't lose hope, don't give up, and
don't give in! It's not over until God says so. Like the woman in Luke
13:10-17, who was bent for 18 years, many thought she couldn't be
made straight, but Jesus proved them wrong when He saw her and
had compassion on her. He called her forward, laid hands on her, and
immediately she was straightened up.

Whatever your challenge is, however long it may be, it can
change. You can change for the better, so let nothing hinder you from
achieving God's best. There is no circumstance that God cannot call
back to life. There is nothing too hard or crooked for God to straight-
en out. Allow your 'bent state of being' to launch you into your purpose. So, position yourself to be straightened up, and position yourself to be realigned by God.

PRAYER

Lord, thank You for Your grace upon me and within my life. Help me to understand that time is in Your hands. Help me to not be stifled by my bent state of being, but to endure and trust Your will for my life. Help me to understand that my victory is ahead, and though I may be bent, I am unbreakable; for greater is He that is in me than he that is in the world. Amen.

Who Are you Fighting?

~ Patrice Reid ~

"For we are not fighting against flesh-and-blood enemies, but against evil rulers and authorities of the unseen world, against mighty powers in this dark world, and against evil spirits in the heavenly places." - Ephesians 6:12, NLV

There is a war that is being fought every single day of our lives; whether we realize it or not, it is happening. There is a war in the spirit as much as there is on earth. You see, we have an enemy of our soul who has made it his number one mission to kill, steal and destroy the human race and stop us from living the life that Jesus died for us to live. A life filled with love, hope, faith, peace, and abundance in God. Many of us have been fighting battles in our family, culture, education, careers, relationships, and even in our faith. There is always a force that seems to want to keep us bound, so we struggle to make ends meet and live as God intended for us to live.

Have you ever had a light bulb moment, an eye-opening experience of who you are and your purpose on earth? Then suddenly, out of nowhere, this strong resistance of doubt, anxiety, and fear starts to overtake your mind

"What just happened here?"
"Where is all this coming from?"
"Why am I feeling this way?"
"Is something wrong with me?"
"Why do I feel stuck?"

And the questions go on and on, and the confidence you once had in your purpose, call, career, relationships, family, ministry, and life is all lost in one moment, and it's like it never happened. This is because we have an enemy of our soul (will, mind, and emotions), who is working overtime, to ensure we stay stuck, confused and lack faith in our Creator. In Genesis 3, he questioned Eve out of her place of abundance, confidence, and security in the Father. The enemy even approached Jesus, our Lord and Savior, and challenged Him with His own words... he is no respect of persons, and he is very consistent and persistent in his pursuit to destroy us.

The Bible reminds us we are in a war, and we must arm ourselves with the protection that God has given us according to Ephesians 6:12 (KJV), "For we are not fighting against flesh-and-blood enemies, but against evil rulers and authorities of the unseen world, against mighty powers in this dark world, and against evil spirits in the heavenly places." We don't fight against family, government, spouses, or educational systems but an enemy that has been lying and deceiving so many from the beginning of time. And so we must be dressed and armored for war and fight from a place where we are seated in a heavenly place in Christ Jesus according to Ephesians 2:6.

PRAYER

Thank You, Lord Jesus, that we are seated with You in heavenly places and that we don't fight with just any weapon. In 2 Cor. 10:2, Your word says, "The weapons of our warfare are not physical [weapons of flesh and blood]." Our weapons are divinely powerful for the destruction of fortresses. And so we use them today in the name of Jesus to destroy every lie and trick of the enemy coming against us and our destiny. Holy Spirit, help me to continue to walk fully armored in God and live a life full of faith, courage, and love, in Jesus' name Amen!

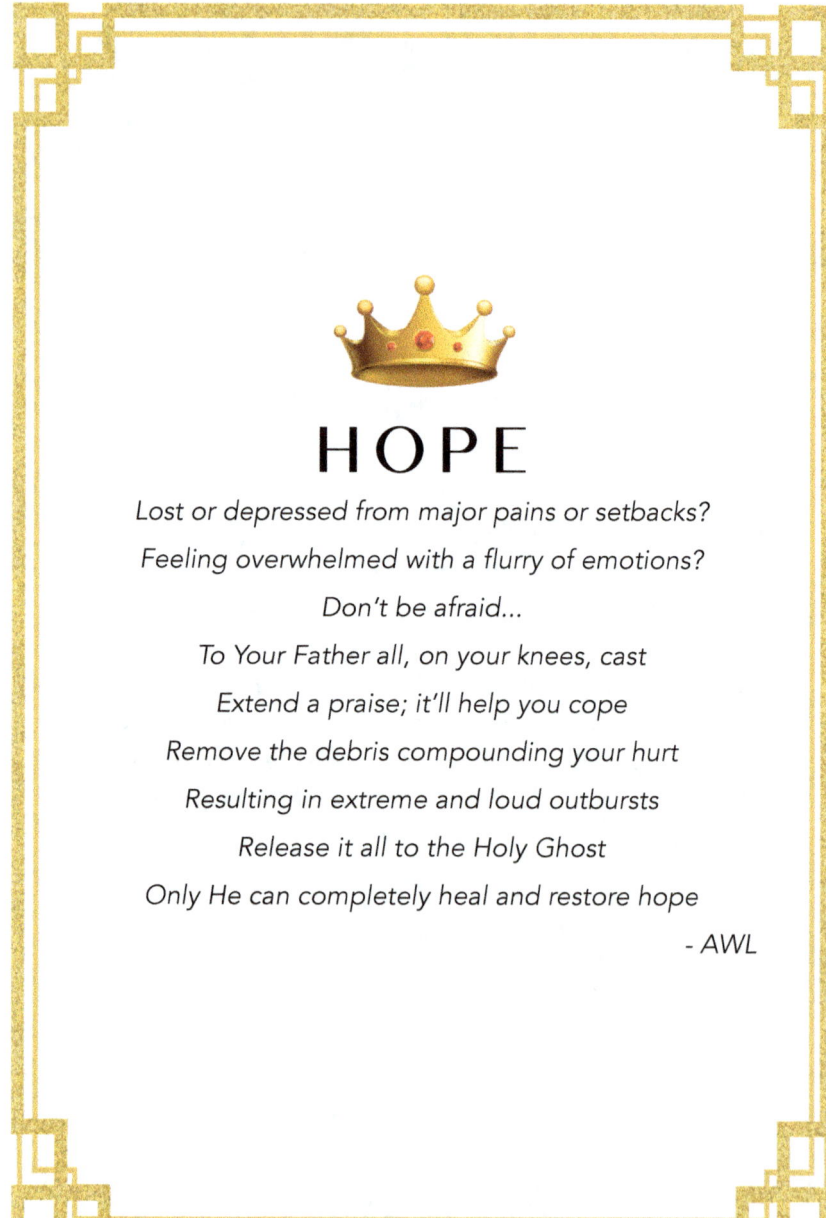

HOPE

Lost or depressed from major pains or setbacks?
Feeling overwhelmed with a flurry of emotions?
Don't be afraid...
To Your Father all, on your knees, cast
Extend a praise; it'll help you cope
Remove the debris compounding your hurt
Resulting in extreme and loud outbursts
Release it all to the Holy Ghost
Only He can completely heal and restore hope

- AWL

You're Not Alone

~ Lacyann Nation ~

"Have I not commanded you? Be strong and courageous. Do not be frightened, and do not be dismayed, for the Lord your God is with you wherever you go."
- Joshua 1:9, ESV

Have you ever felt like there is so much going on in your life, and you don't know where to turn or what to do? Have you ever been so down that you don't know if you will ever be able to get up again?

Going through life, we face many struggles that make us wonder why we were selected for the suffering. We sometimes believe we are the only ones struggling, and no one else would understand. Well, I am here to tell you: you're not alone.

It is in times like these that we turn to God and our sisters and brothers in Christ. God is always there for us. He is never too busy for us, and He is never avoiding our calls. While our friends or families may get tired of us, God never does and is always there. He is just waiting for us to call out to Him and lay all our burdens, fears, and doubts on Him. He will bear it all for us. All He asks is that we have faith and trust in Him. God sees us when we are struggling, but we need to realize He is the one we can turn to. Once we understand that, we can pray and open our hearts to receive what He has for us. Once we have received what God has for us, we need to stay in His presence through prayer because we do not want to fall back into that place of feeling alone. We need to remember God is omnipresent, so He is always with us...you're not alone!

PRAYER

Father, I feel alone in these trials that I face, but today I turn to You here and now because I know I don't have to be alone. You're always there with me to guide and protect me. From now on, I will always put my faith and trust in You. I open my heart to receive all You have ordained for me. Saying thanks, in Jesus' name. Amen.

Broken to Be a Blessing

~ Andre Weir-Leach ~

"We are hard-pressed on every side, yet not crushed; we are per-plexed, but not in despair. Persecuted, but not forsaken, struck down but not destroyed..." - 2 Corinthians 4:8-9, KJV

"Broken and bruised, maybe refused, you do not have to remain in those shoes. Life may not be a cruise, but these experiences you can use; to help others relieve their blues."

As I sat to write a paper, I was immediately sent into some deep reflections. I had some very heart-rending flashbacks of me mentor-ing youths, encouraging, and helping total strangers, who at times just walked up to me and began pouring out. I thought to myself, how could I help them and not break down, having also walked in some of those very shoes?

I, too, had experienced losses, like the death of my dad in my early teens, among other things. But with the help of family and friends, I was able to manage to some extent. There were deeper pains beyond their reach. At times, I felt ambushed and helpless. Thank God I learned to pray from an early age; I would cry out to God every now and then which led me to realize how much He cared for me. I began to feel His presence, love, and peace. This drew me closer to Him and helped me release all to Him.

Over time, I realized that people were drawn to me because of God's special deposit inside me. This shone through and caused others to see beyond my smile. He also gave me a kind heart, the ability to listen attentively, and the wisdom to use my very past to give advice to help others improve their situations. God and His angels surrounded me — they were my wall of defense.

Many times, we despise and see our circumstances, failures, and pains as stumbling blocks. However, God wants us to know that our bad experiences in life are not there to crush our spirit. These should strengthen us and testify of His mercy and love in us. I overcame by trusting God and casting all my cares on Jesus in good and bad times. Guess what, you can too. I don't know what you've been through, but for sure, I know God understands and can help you get through.

Remember, God is your protector and even though you're aching now, there is hope after the pain.

Unburden yourself, lean into God, study and apply His words – therein lies your healing. You too, can be a blessing despite your bruising – for where Christ dwells, this same Ministry is present! Intentionally become more with the joy He provides after the breaking.

Declare: "Where there has been grief, He will bring joy. "Gladness and joy will overtake you, and sorrow and sighing will flee away." (Isaiah 51:11, KJV)

PRAYER

Lord Jesus, please, help me to get past my pains and experience your joy. Surround me with Your holy angels and presence as I cast every care on You. I trust You to see me through, so I can be a blessing to others too. Thank You for Your healing. Amen.

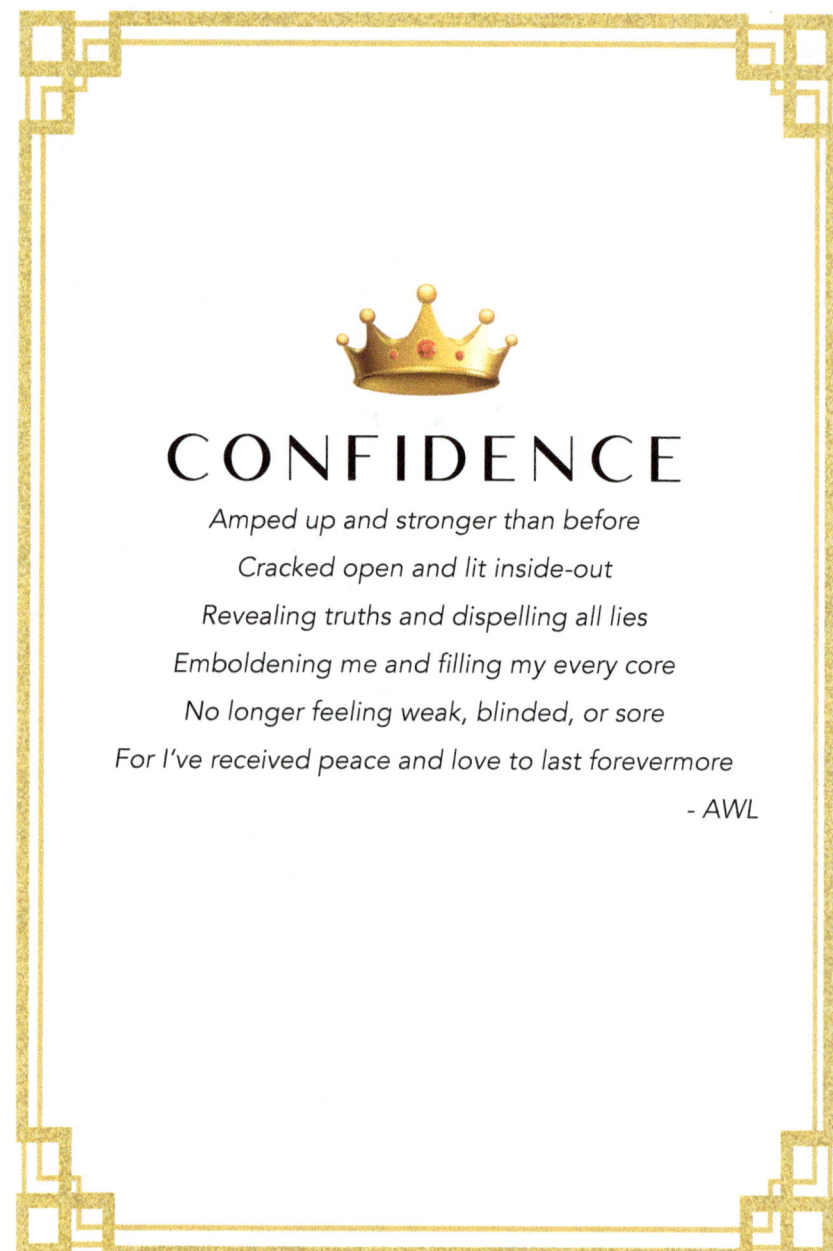

CONFIDENCE

Amped up and stronger than before

Cracked open and lit inside-out

Revealing truths and dispelling all lies

Emboldening me and filling my every core

No longer feeling weak, blinded, or sore

For I've received peace and love to last forevermore

- AWL

"Trust God and Live"

~ Patrice Reid ~

"But blessed are those who trust in the LORD and have made the LORD their hope and confidence."
- Jeremiah 17:7, NLT

As we go through the different seasons of life storms, unexpected turbulences will arise. Only those out there who hope and trust in God will see the sunshine at the end. Our relationships are often tested, especially when someone whom we know and love betrays us. Even our very relationship with God at times is tested because of the things we believed God for that didn't work out in our favor. It could be that our health starts to fail or even a reduction in the finances that we were hoping for.

Life is fickle! I can remember going through some very rough times financially, and I just couldn't figure out how or what was happening. I tithed from what I had and gave my talent and time in ministry and other areas, but I still struggled to reach my financial goals. I needed a car and believed that I wouldn't experience any trouble getting a new one after years of serving others with it. There were even times when it broke down in the middle of taking some youths home after church. Losing my car was the last thing I needed to happen at that time because I knew it meant more pressure on an already over-exhausted bank account and budget.

To be honest, I felt a little embarrassed even though I knew what the Word of God said. But it was a great opportunity for me to "Trust God and Live!" You see, it is in moments like these that we must "trust God and live."

When it gets dark and things are unclear in our thoughts, it's important that we change our very attitude about what's really happening and declare, "I trust You, Lord." In these moments, the Word of God must become our antidote to combat the lies of lack and poverty in our lives.

55

PRAYER

Lord, I thank You for the power and life of Your Word. It is truly Spirit and Life. I thank You that Your Word reminds us in Jeremiah 17:7(NLT), "Blessed are those who trust in the LORD and have made the LORD their hope and confidence." Lord, for everyone reading this today, I pray they will see that even in their seasons of great need, they can trust You and live, knowing that we serve a God of time and great wonder. You will come through for them, and they will rejoice in the God of their salvation. All this, I pray in Jesus' name. Amen.

Launch Out into the Deep

~ Shanae Clarke ~

"Now when he had left speaking, he said unto Simon, Launch out into the deep, and let down your nets for a draught. And Simon answering said unto him, Master, we have toiled all the night, and have taken nothing: nevertheless at thy word I will let down the net."
- Luke 5:4-5, KJV

In Luke 5, Jesus is by the Sea of Galilee, and He sees two empty ships by the seashore and the fishermen nearby washing their nets. He instructs Simon to launch his boat back out into the deep waters and let down his nets. Previously, Simon and his brother, Andrew, had worked all night and caught nothing. Simon could have followed his feelings and said no after the rough night he had, but he took Jesus up on His invitation, drew his boat back into the water, and let down his net. His obedience to Jesus' instruction led to an abundant catch that was even too much for his nets to contain.

The phrase "Launch out into the Deep" is an invitation to go deeper — to discover something new. And for these men, Jesus was saying, I know that you're tired, but trust me and witness what I will do. God desires that we become mature sons and daughters. When Jesus came, He revealed God as Father, and when He was leaving, He said that it was good that He should go away because if He didn't, the Comforter would not come (John 16:7, KJV). Jesus says that when the Holy Spirit comes, He will lead them into all truth (John 16:13, KJV). There are so many things that the Lord wants to reveal to us, but it depends on us relinquishing control.

From the inception of our Christian journey, God has been calling us to launch out. Upon hearing the message of the Gospel, we felt that stirring in our hearts from the Holy Spirit to surrender to Him. Our eyes become open to our sins and how it separates us from God, so we receive Him as Savior. In following Him as Savior, we then became His disciples. As His disciples, we learned that we had to deny ourselves, pick up our cross, and follow Him. In surrendering everything to Him, we discover Him as a loving Father who is good, rich in love, and slow to anger. And in receiving Him as Father, we also have to prepare to meet Him again as the Bridegroom who will one day come back for His church.

Practically speaking, one thing that has helped me to grow in my relationship with God is PRAYER. In Paul's letters to the churches in the New Testaments, he always issued a prayer to strengthen and deepen the faith of the believers. Ephesians 1: 17-19, for example, is one that I use in my prayer time when I am simply asking God to increase my capacity for more of Him. As you make the decision to launch out, apply this: ASK, SEEK, KNOCK and remember this simple kingdom principle: our God is not a respecter of persons.

PRAYER

Dear God,

Give me a desire to pursue You more. I don't want to only know about Your deeds, I want to know Your ways. I want to grow in my relationship with You. As the Holy Spirit reveals the truth of who You are and what You have called me to do, my "yes" to You will not only impact my life for the better but also, the generations to come. I pray that wherever You lead me, I will follow without hesitation. Amen.

GIFTS

Revealed and yet sometimes concealed,

Rare and exquisite with attractions like a magnet

Precious skills which most have put to chill

Afraid to release so it can send thrills of joy and peace.

- AWL

Treasure Within

~ Tecora Noble ~

"But we have this treasure in earthen vessels..."
- 2 Corinthians 4:7, KJV

When we think about "treasures," we normally think about something tangible, like a precious gem or items of great value. So, if I told you that, as a daughter of the King, you hold the most precious and valuable treasure any man could ever desire, one that's not tangible and is not a gem but is more precious than silver or gold, would you believe me?

Well, 2 Timothy 1:14 (AMP) says, "Guard and keep unchanged, the treasure which has been entrusted to you through the help of the Holy Spirit who dwells in you."

In short, God wants you to protect His precious truth with all that's within you! He wants you to watch over the good news of salvation, which He has committed to you and your care, not by yourself but in collaboration with His indwelling spirit and faith in Him. The good news of Jesus is your treasure. Not everyone has or will receive this treasure, but anyone can. This treasure cannot be hoarded to oneself. It needs to be shared with friends, family, neighbors, and strangers.

What is the good news you know? Well, it's Jesus Christ, the Son of the True Living God, who came to earth, died for our sins, and was resurrected from the dead. Today, I am now living by grace, and I want us to know that when we understand and accept the Gospel of Jesus, we become a treasured possession, holding a treasure. Deuteronomy 14:2 (ESC) states, "You are a people, holy to the Lord your God, and the Lord has "chosen" you to be a people for his treasured possessions, out of all the people who are on the face of the earth."

So, we are not only chosen but blessed! We are blessed because we have received knowledge by and through the Holy Spirit of Jesus Christ.

Proverbs 3:13-15 (ESV) states, "Blessed is the one who finds wisdom and the one who gets understanding for the gain from her is better than silver and her profit better than gold. She is more precious than jewels, and nothing you desire can compare with her."

We, therefore, say that when we possess God's treasure, we are richer! God's fear is now within us, granting us knowledge. The Holy Spirit within us will teach us all things and remind us of everything. He who dwells within us will keep us grounded and alert. The Holy Spirit is this "true treasure within" that no man can buy. He is a rare gem, the only one of its kind, and only those who accept Jesus (the way, the truth, and life) can and will receive Him.

PRAYER

Abba Father, who art in heaven, hallowed be Your name. Thank You for Your Son, Jesus Christ, who allowed me to receive this great treasure of the Gospel. Help me to treasure Your presence more than anything I might place a high value on. Allow me, Lord, to use Your spirit as a treasure not only for my benefits but for those who need to find You, in Jesus' name. Amen.

Your Gift

~ Shauna-Kay Calder ~

"For this reason, I remind you to fan into flame the gift of God,
which is in you through the laying on of my hands."
- 2 Timothy 1:6, NIV

Paul, Timothy's mentor and good friend, gives Timothy this encouragement as he faces this tough situation. "For this reason, I remind you to fan into flame the gift of God, which is in you through the laying on of my hand" (2 Timothy 1:6, NIV). You get the image. You've had a fire, but the flame is dying. But you're not ready to call it a night, so you get down on your knees and blow on it. Then, you rearrange the dying embers, add more wood, and get the fire going again. It's amazing.

I don't think Paul is necessarily saying that Timothy had let his fire die down. I think Paul is putting his finger on a problem that all of us have, even in normal times, but especially when we face tough times. Things naturally die down. Whatever you don't maintain and invest in gradually dies. Nothing stays in pristine shape by itself. If you want to grow something, you need to invest in it.

What does Paul say to rekindle? There's a unique application to Timothy, but this applies to all of us. Paul and other elders had set Timothy apart for a special role in ministry. To formally recognize this moment, they laid hands on him to appoint him into service.

So, there's a special application in this command to Timothy, but the same principle applies to all of us because if you are a follower of Jesus Christ, you have been given a ministry and gifts from the Holy Spirit. The Bible teaches that God gives every believer a special gift through His grace — He uses the gift to extend His grace and love to others through you. You don't earn it. You can't gain it. There's no way you can get it on your own. There's nothing you can do to deserve it. But, God gives every believer the gift that the Holy Spirit sovereignly wants to give. When you use that, God enables you through the Holy Spirit so that you do more than you would be able to do on your own.

God has given you something the rest of us need, and you need to rekindle it regularly. How do you do this? Use it. Pray about it. Invest in it. Be intentional with it.

Think about this for a minute. We often talk about turning to Jesus, repentance and faith, and God forgiving your past, remaking you in the present, and guaranteeing your future. That's what it means to follow Jesus. We turn to Him with empty hands of faith, and He transforms us, and we follow Him for the rest of our lives.

If you have never done that before, you can do that right now. Turn to Him with your mess, and receive the gift of forgiveness and transformation because of what Jesus has done for you. But there's more than even what I just described.

When we turn to God in repentance and faith, He gives us a spiritual gift — the ability empowered by the Holy Spirit to be used to extend His love and grace to others. If you have followed Jesus, it's not possible for you not to have a spiritual gift. He's given you something that the rest of us need. Use it!

God intends to use you. You may think, I have nothing to offer. That may be exactly the feeling Timothy faced — feeling inadequate and unequal to the challenges before him. But, Paul reminded him that God had given him a gift, and it would go out unless he rekindled it. Use your gifts, or you will lose them. An untended fire will die. It's easy to be scared and to feel inadequate, but God intends to use you. For some, it will require stepping out and doing something you've never done before. For others, it will involve staying faithful.

Keep going! Keep rekindling the flame! Keep using that gift, prayerfully asking for God's help as you do so. Don't let it go out. I wish I could look every one of you in the eyes and give you this encouragement. God has given you a gift. He desires to extend His love and grace to others through you. He needs you to use your gift! It's within you; it's something you drift towards because it's how God has shaped you.

Some of you may be thinking you don't know what gift you have. I have two pieces of advice for you. First, ask around. Other people probably see your gift more clearly than you do. Second, the Bible never tells us to worry very much about figuring out what gift we have. It just tells us to get serving.

Where you feel drawn to serve is probably a reflection of where God has gifted you. Some of you love encouraging and showing mercy to others. That's your gift! Some of you love organizing and providing leadership. That's what God has given you! Some of you love to serve. Some of you love to teach. Whatever it is, stir that into flame.

You can usually tell what it is because you have a desire to do it, and usually, you get feedback from others that God uses you in a unique way when you do it. Don't let fear or apathy shut that down. Rekindle it. It's one of the reasons God has put you here. We need it! We need it always, but we especially need it now. God has given you a ministry, a purpose, and we need it! That's the encouragement that Paul gave to Timothy, and it's the encouragement that I want to give to you today.

PRAYER

Eternal God, equip me with all I need to enter into my place of power, which is in You. Help me not to see prayer as a burden but instead as a burden lifter. As I do the natural, Spirit of the living God, I ask that You do the SUPER in me by Your power and awaken my gifts within me. Father, I want to bloom where I am planted and resist the temptation to compare myself to others. Help me see the ways You have uniquely gifted me to serve You and Your Kingdom. Thank You for making me just as I am. Forgive me for the ways I have compared myself and coveted the abilities of others. I pray that starting today, I will see the opportunities in front of me to use my gifts and abilities. Help me to do great exploits for You and greatly impact my generation, in Jesus' name, I pray. Amen.

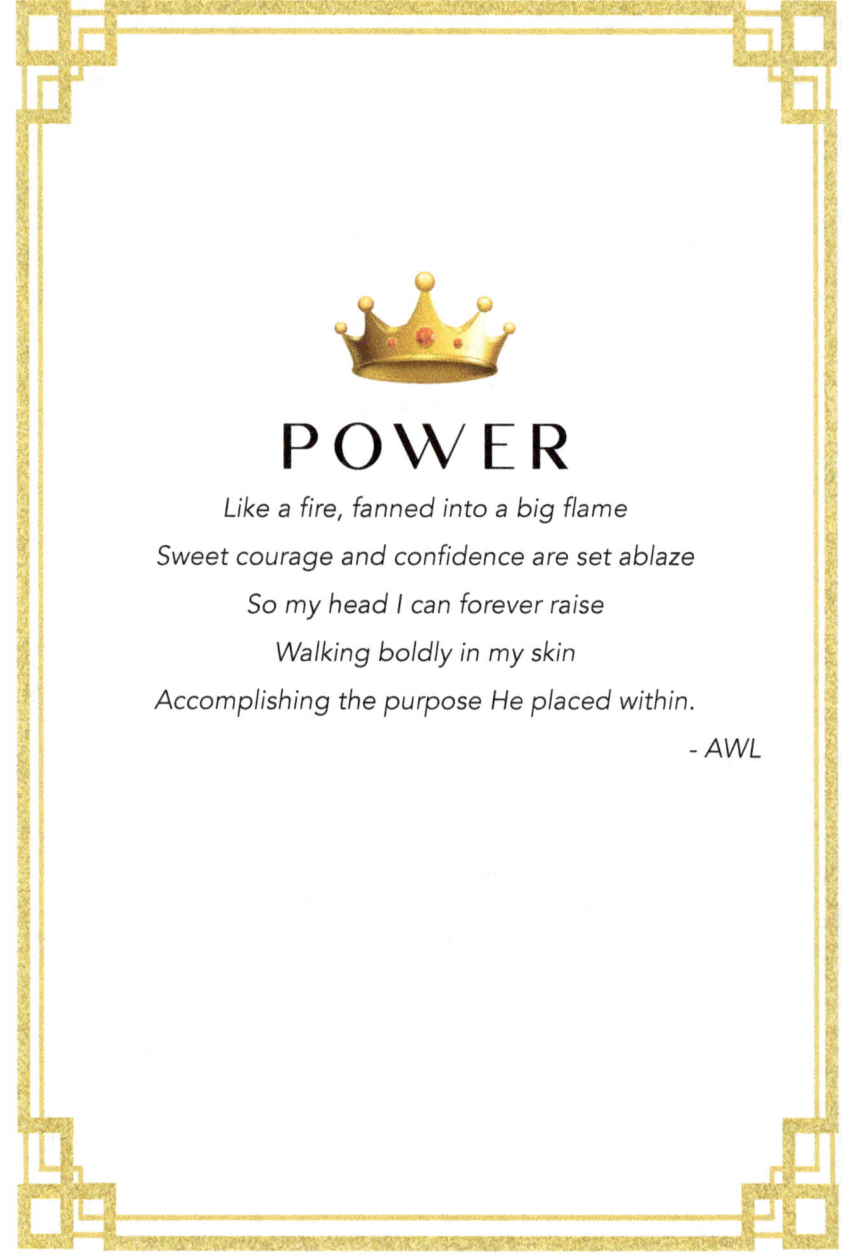

POWER

Like a fire, fanned into a big flame

Sweet courage and confidence are set ablaze

So my head I can forever raise

Walking boldly in my skin

Accomplishing the purpose He placed within.

- AWL

The Power Within

~ Tecora Noble ~

"And if the Spirit of him who raised Jesus from the dead is living in you, he who raised Christ from the dead will also give life to your mortal bodies because of his Spirit who lives in you."
- Romans 8:11, NIV

As a little girl, I enjoyed watching superheroes, especially Superwoman and Wonder Woman. They were beautiful and powerful, and that caught my attention. I was fascinated by their abilities and confidence. And even though they were fictional characters, I wanted to be like them. That was then. Today, I can say I possess a power, not like theirs, but greater! No longer do I have to pine after theirs or wonder about it!

"So, what power?" You might ask. - It is the power of the Holy Spirit. The supernatural power of the Holy Spirit transforms each of us into a new creation, spiritually, mentally, and physically. We are able to heal ourselves and others, speak life into dead situations, and give sight to the blind.

I can also tell you that you can possess this great power, too. If you have already accepted Jesus, then you already have it. If you have not, you can accept Him and receive this great power within you. This power that Jesus gives surpasses that of both Superwoman and Wonder Woman. 1 John 4:4 (KJV) tells us, "Greater is He that is in you than he that is in the world." God is the God of the impossible. You can do the impossible through the power of the Holy Spirit that dwells within you.

Romans 8:11 reminds us that the same power that raised Jesus from the dead lives in us. Oh, what power we possess as God's children! Though many would doubtfully ask, "How can you raise the dead?" I have no doubt that the power which raised Lazarus and Jesus from the dead can raise the dead now.

Our God Almighty is still in the business of resurrection. He can raise up and awaken every dead situation in your life right now. As His child, you can command your dead situations to enter the land of the living and command every brokenness to be made whole again! You have that power once you have received Jesus, the Savior and mighty Deliverer. You don't need any extravagant outfit to prove you have this power. Proverbs 31:25 (AMP) says, "Strength and dignity are her clothing, and her position is strong and secure." As a child of God, you are clothed in His righteousness because He is righteous. You are powerful and anointed with His strength.

Have you ever noticed in the movies that when superheroes are disinclined to use their powers, nothing but chaos happens around them? Their reluctance to take authority and use their power causes the enemy to prevail more, getting away with all kinds of crimes. It's just constant mayhem! Well, that's the same way it is when you do not use the power of the Holy Spirit that is vested in you. The enemy seems to become more rampant, constantly scheming up and rearing his ugly head. The enemy is always watching, waiting, and ready to kill, steal and destroy. The very reason God has given you His Spirit is so that when the devil sees you, he will flee.

Remember, you are here to be victorious! You have His indwelling power, and you are a conqueror. You can empower with your words and bring forth life because "death and life are in the power of your tongue" (Proverbs 18:21, AMP).

You are here to save others who are being held captive in their minds, who are sick in their bodies, and dead in their trespasses and sins. The Holy Spirit is ready to be used by you, so rise up, stand firm as a soldier of the Lord, and use your power. Be bold, my sister. All-powerful is His name.

PRAYER

Abba Father, who art in heaven, hallowed be Your name. Thank You for Your Sovereign Spirit that dwells in me. Help me understand that Your supernatural power is greater than my comprehension, and help me to use it for Your glory. In Jesus' mighty name. Amen.

God's Resources

~ Shauna-Kay Calder ~

"For God gave us a spirit not of fear but of power and love and self-control." – 2 Timothy 1:7, ESV

If you are fearful, God did not give you that. Fear isn't one of the resources that God hands out with spiritual gifts. You did not get that from Him.

Here are the three things God has given you:
- *power*
- *love*
- *self-control*

If you need the power to serve God, He will give it. If you need love, which is important for all ministry, that's His specialty. He'll give you all the love you need. If you need discipline and self-control, God will give you that, too. He will give you everything you need to use your spiritual gifts to bless others. Not only does God give you the gift, but He also gives you everything you need to use that gift. Listen, my friends, I began by asking you what you're afraid of. We all struggle with fear. Timothy did. We do, too.

But then Paul tells Timothy, and indirectly he tells us, too — don't let fear get in the way of God using the gift He's given you to show His love to others. Not only has God given you a gift, but He's given you everything you need to use that gift. We must apply ourselves to use that gift with the resources God has given us. It may actually be one of the best ways to move past fear like Timothy did. Remember your calling and use the gifts that God has given you to bless others.

PRAYER

Lord, fear and apathy are natural to all of us. It has a way of shutting us down. Thank You for the reminder today that even in tough times, You've given us all an assignment. You've given us something to do. You don't just call us to You; You give us a ministry so that You can use us to bless others. And then You give us everything we need to carry that ministry out. Help us to rekindle that flame. And help us to tap into Your power, love, and self-control so that we can carry out that assignment. We pray this in Jesus' name. Amen.

DETERMINATION

Listen to God and rise above all odds

Realize the force at each course

Spring into form, remain calm

Eyes focused on Christ more than the prize

Though you realize, the force and depth within that lies

Slow, steadfast steps truly are best

In staying the path and winning each test

Victory bed is where you'll eventually rest

- AWL

I Must Live

~ Patrice Reid ~

"I shall not die, but live, and declare the works of the LORD."
- Psalm 118:17, KJV

I woke up from a dream with the mouth of a gun pressed against my forehead. It felt so real. It was as if the person was standing in my room. I could feel the impact and impression, and the only thing left for them to do was pull the trigger. Darkness filled the room, but I noticed that I wasn't fearful. Instead, it was like I was at ease, wondering what was coming next.

One of the strange things was at the beginning of the dream. I was preaching to a group of individuals, and as soon as we finished, this man walked in and came directly to me as if he knew just who I was. He went through my small purse with my money, cards, and a few receipts and then walked away. But immediately after walking away, he turned around and pulled out a gun, and with astonishment, I just stood there.

As I mentioned earlier, the mouth of the gun was pressed so hard against my forehead I could feel it even after I woke up. As I stood there waiting for whatever this hitman in the spirit was about to do, I heard "YOU MUST LIVE" with such a strong tone. I woke up and shouted, "YES! I MUST LIVE!" Then the Holy Ghost reminded me of Psalm 118:17 (KJV), "I shall not die, but live. And declare the works of the LORD." I became so empowered just declaring the Word of the Lord that I now realized that only the Word of God could destroy the wicked works of the enemy.

You might be wondering why I am sharing this dream? It was just a dream... But let me tell you, the dream world is as real as the waking world. There is a real enemy that will stop at nothing to destroy you, even in your dream. But he will come in one way and flee several ways when using the Word as your weapon.

PRAYER

Lord Jesus, You declared that man shall not live by bread alone but by every Word that proceeds from the mouth of God. Lord, as we go through this life, many will be the attacks, betrayals, and hurt, but Your Word is Spirit, and it is Life and will heal, deliver, and protect us no matter what. Thank You, Lord, in Jesus' name, Amen!

Stay Anchored

~ Andre Weir-Leach ~

"Which hope we have as an anchor to the soul, both sure and stead-fast, and which enters into that within the veil."
- Hebrews 6:19, KJV

One afternoon, while at home meditating on God's Word, He whispered the word "anchored" to me. I repeated it, and then He said, "Stay Anchored." It kept resonating with me, and I said ok, then began probing my mind for words similar to anchor. Thoughts like cement, ground yourself, stand firm, stay strong, and get rooted began to surface. Then I remembered my very first severe wind chill on my way to work one morning in Japan.

I had just exited the bus and was hit by a fierce, cold wind; my head and body swayed back. I literally had to brace myself and muster up the courage to make it to the school gate. I wrapped my scarf a little tighter around my neck and face but thought, 'Oh, I need more attire to help combat this.' I quickly said a little prayer inside and started the trek, taking careful steps to ground my feet. As I walked, the winds seemed to get more boisterous; I swayed even more, hugging myself and stopping a couple of times to regain my footing and strength to continue. I finally made it safely to the gate and inside the compound, thanking God I didn't get blown away.

This experience is also a reminder of our walk with God. Let's be honest. There truly is no red carpet or plush pillows! At times, life throws some serious blows like those wild winds I experienced. So wild, they rock your very core, trying to weaken your faith and foundation, but you have to know how to react.

Sometimes, you need to just stop and regroup via prayer and fasting, speaking the scriptures out aloud or inwardly to strengthen you or simply sing some praises unto God (Ephesians 5:19, KJV). The most effective thing you can do is wrap yourself in God and submit all to Him. Anchoring yourself more in Him during these horrific times will help to shield you. So next time rowdy winds blow your way, don't delve in nose-deep or allow your emotions to lead. Instead, let God guide you to dance through, creating rhythmic victory beats with your feet.

PRAYER

Dear God, forgive me for allowing life's storms to shake my core. Help me to remember in times like these, You become more than just my Hope. You are my Rock; allowing me to come through unscathed. Thank You for being my help and anchor each day. I pray for strength of mind and determination as I anchor my soul afresh in You today. In Jesus' mighty name, Amen.

Stay the Course

~ Andre Weir-Leach ~

"Therefore, my beloved brethren, be ye steadfast, unmovable, always abounding in the work of the Lord, forasmuch as ye know that your labor is not in vain in the Lord."
- 1 Corinthians 15:58, KJV

Do you ever replay some of the things you read in a favorite book? Well, I sometimes do, especially when it's a good book with a great plot and storyline with similar things I've experienced.

Now, as a child growing up, I enjoyed reading books about mysteries and adventures. One such adventure book was Robinson Crusoe. After a while, I also developed a liking for cricket because my mom was so patriotic and never missed a season to cheer for her favorite team. Finally, one year while trying to recover from an asthma attack, I succumbed to the game. I became so engulfed and, quite surprisingly, started cheering inwardly with her despite my pains.

Like Robinson Crusoe, I saw in this team great determination. It was amazing to see that after batting in successive innings and not reaching their target runs, it never dampened their spirits much. They still gave it their all and sometimes arose champions. They had a deep desire to win and fought hard despite the pressures and odds they encountered, just like their enthusiastic supporters.

I remember thinking, No! when I witnessed some very depressing plays and scores. Yet, they wowed me by managing to leave the field with smiles and sometimes return with such great force to crush their opponents. On the other hand, Robinson Crusoe dreamt of journeying like his brothers on the sea but was subjected to a journey of self-discovery through his association with nature. He struggled with winds and storms of disobedience, quarrels and sufferings yet arose, revealing God's grace and mercy plus true survival.

When I think of us as believers, though true, I feel ashamed to say that we give up too easily at times. We sometimes forget what God has done and is capable of. We should have not the same but a greater determination and desire to win, despite the storms of life. Our opponent, Lucifer, fights really dirty and hard, never giving up. If we only realize who we are and the power that lies within us, we can overcome and overpower anything he sends our way. We need to keep our eyes focused on our Father, pressing toward the high calling in Jesus (Philippians 3:1-4, KJV) and, as Paul also says, running to obtain (1 Corinthians 9:24, KJV).

Yes, there may be times when you get knocked down or falter but be like that cricket team; **never give up hope.** Dismiss any resemblance of fear, and fight the good fight of faith (Philippians 6:11, KJV) by remaining faithful to your ministry and calling in Christ. I know God will finish what He started in you; believe and walk in it (Philippians 1:6, KJV). Someone needs to witness your determination to help them hurdle their struggles too.

PRAYER

Mighty God, I ask You to forgive me for all those times I surrendered to my storms and thought I was weak. Grant me a determined spirit and mind to press through. I commit my all to You and pray that my faith will be strengthened too. Thank You, Jesus, for always believing in and being there for me, Amen.

PURPOSED

Unlocking the power within

Finding God and submitting to His will

Walking with meaning, confidently speaking

Inspiring others and encouraging

As you seek to succeed at what you've been dreaming

But most importantly, what Your Father's revealing

Realizing the talents and time you've been lent

Are worth sharing with great intent

As you experience great accomplishments

- AWL

Purposed for Good

~ Andre Weir-Leach ~

"For we are His workmanship, created in Christ Jesus unto good works, which God prepared beforehand, that we should walk in them." - Ephesians 2:10, KJV

As I stood combing my hair and talking with my younger daughter, she told me about her three main wishes for the world. One of them struck me more than the others. She wished there were no spiders in the world.

With knitted brows, I turned and asked, "Why?"
She replied, "I don't like them. I am afraid of them."
I explained, "Everything has a purpose in this world, even if we find some of it scary."

I briefly shared some info about the ecosystem and how spiders play a critical role in controlling the insect populations so that we can have more food. She was surprised. Her eyes and face beamed with interest, and a few questions followed about our purpose as humans. So, I told her that our main purpose as humans was to fear God and keep His commandments (Ecclesiastes 12:13, KJV). However, we each have a natural and spiritual purpose unique to us, like the spider. This purpose was ordained by God to help our fellow men and the world be a better place.

She began to think carefully about her purpose. I had to leave for work, so I concluded by telling her that God revealed to many biblical characters their true purpose, and she should ask Him about hers. Psalm 139:13-18 (KJV), tells us, "He knitted us together in the womb, He knows us inside-out, our days upon the land, and from Him nothing about us is hidden."

We were all predestined for good, but, like my daughter, are you unaware of your true purpose? Do you know and want to fulfill your purpose in life? Consider the ant or spider. If they, as creatures so small, have a purpose and fulfill it, what say you and me? Take some time to reflect, then ask God to reveal your unique purpose.

Do you fully accept what He has shown you? Are you ready or already walking in your purpose?

PRAYER

Father God and Creator of all, before I existed, You gave me a purpose; reveal it to me, I pray. I know my destiny belongs to You, and I desire to walk with and glorify You. I humbly submit my will to You, so Your purpose can be fulfilled in me. Thank You, Jesus, for hearing and answering, Amen.

I Will Answer the Call

~ Lacyann Nation ~

"Now the Lord said to Abram, 'Go from your country and your kindred and your father's house to the land that I will show you.'"
- Genesis 12:1, ESV

Do you wonder what it is that the Lord has planned for you? How many times have you started doing things because you think you know what God wants for you? God has a calling on all our lives, but we have to answer that call. Not according to what we think or want but based on what God has shown us personally or has spoken through one of His messengers. Sometimes what we want does not align with what God wants for us. So, the question is, will you answer the call when you're called?

I am a child of God. I know He has a calling on my life. What that calling is, I was not certain. He has blessed me to be a nurse, and He has blessed me to do special prayers for others whenever I get the inkling to do so. The thing is, while I love to pray for others, you would never hear me pray out loud or write a personal prayer to anyone when I feel the urge to do so. I would let the person know that I would pray for them and then do so in silence.

I have found that sometimes it is necessary to pray out loud or write a personal prayer to someone, especially when God wants to speak to others through you. Now, I have prayed for God to crucify the spirit of fear and doubt that has kept me from doing it. I have answered the call that Christ has on my life, and I will walk in it with boldness and confidence. Like Abram did in the Bible, we have to be obedient to His call.

PRAYER

Lord, I come before You on bended knees, asking for You to reveal to me Your calling on my life. Help me to cast away any fears that may be hindering me from answering Your call. Amen.

Living Legacy

~ Andre Weir-Leach ~

"We will not hide them from their children, but tell to the coming generation the glorious deeds of the LORD, and his might, and the wonders that he has done."
- Psalm 78:4, ESV

"A good man leaves an inheritance to his children's children, but the sinner's wealth is laid up for the righteous."
- Proverbs 13:22, ESV

Being a child of the King, legacy (to me) means so much more than leaving an inheritance of money for my loved ones. I want my legacy to begin while I'm still alive. I want to strive for excellence and thrive in God so others and my loved ones can see and receive a lesson or two. I want to fully represent the value of life in God, because we cannot truly exist without Him.

We are nothing without God! He is the One who makes all things possible. I want my life to reflect the bounty of life in God revealing that; waking up to an everyday routine is never and will never be enough. Satisfaction in the natural world is only fleeting and temporal. I'm no expert in every field, but my life should be a spiritual flashlight for others.

After much upheaval via sickness and sorrows, I called upon God, and He answered. My life in Christ has made me richer, wiser, and stronger in so many areas. And even though my emotions sometimes get in the way, I choose to rely on God and respond with forgiveness and love.

David was a man after God's own heart, even though he faltered many times. Peter denied Christ, yet he arose as a great minister of the Gospel, healing people and preaching. He lived up to His name as the Rock. Both left a legacy and I will too. I will live purposefully and declare that God is my Hiding Place, Rock, Defense, and Everything! God is my compass; He possesses my reins (Psalm 139:13, KJV).

Like 2020, a year marked as unforgettable in history, we must be determined to live our lives to be just that. We must indelibly mark the paths of many with our lives via faith in God and the application of His words in all we do. As believers, we have the greatest legacy - one born out of our Father's love, determination, and compassion to redeem us. This, He so vividly expressed and passed on to us through His Son. What better legacy can we leave behind if not one of spiritual value, love, and integrity? What better way to honor and display our love to our neighbors and loved ones? (Deuteronomy 6:5-7; Ephesians 6:4, KJV)

PRAYER

Abba Father, You see and know my heart. Transform me to be more like You where I'm lacking, so my legacy to others will be purely You. Let self be slain in all I do, revealing only Your nature and leading many to You. Continue to guide all my thoughts, actions, and speech daily. Let my legacy of You be embossed in all I do, intentional and enduring throughout all generations. In Jesus' mighty name, Amen.

Salvation Prayer

God, in Romans 10:9, your word says, "that if I confess with my mouth the Lord Jesus and believe in my heart that You, God has raised Him from the dead, I will be saved."

Lord Jesus, today I confess my sins and ask for your forgiveness. I believe that you are the Son of God and that you died on the cross to save my soul from destruction. I believe that you rose from the dead and that you are seated at the right hand of the Father daily making intercession for me.

Right now, I surrender my heart and soul to you. I turn from a life of darkness and shame to a life of love, hope and purpose in You. I confess that you are Lord of my life and that my identity is found in you and you alone. I am saved and my life will never be the same again in Jesus' name, Amen.

Daughters of the King

A force propelled her from within
that she never understood
until she decided to accept the "Good."
She walked out of the dark, became a part of,
and was embraced by God's heart.
Then she was hit and lit by truths, not myths.
Forever inspired, to walk with grit
by the greatest Friend
who stays faithfully true to the end.
He gave Himself so she, through Him,
could a new life begin,
helping others experience true awakening.

- AWL

Shauna–Kay Calder

 Shauna-Kay Calder is an ambassador for God. The favor and grace of God have rewritten her life, and for that, she is grateful. She was saved, filled with the Holy Ghost and glad about it. Shauna-Kay is a certified Motivational Speaker and Professional Life Coach encouraging youths and adults to chase after their dreams and take the cap off everything that limits their capacity.

She is a licensed American educator who is intrinsically motivated and driven towards a career in education from two perspectives: as a qualified Elementary teacher holding a Bachelor's Degree in Elementary Education and a Master's Degree in Exceptional Student Education with an endorsement in leadership. Shauna-Kay is enthusiastic and motivated in the classroom because she enjoys nurturing children and providing them with every opportunity to succeed.

Jesus is her flashlight during the dark and bright days!

Proverbs 18:21 tells us that the power of life and death is in our words, and nothing is more powerful than affirming who we are in Christ.

Shanae Clarke

Shanae Clarke was born in Jamaica and came from a family with great love for God and His word. She grew up in the church and knew about the things of God but didn't know Him personally. It wasn't until she was in her mid-20s that she began to pursue a relationship with Jesus wholeheartedly. In surrendering to God's plan for her life, she was led to serve others and worked in Youth and Women's ministry for five years. In serving others, she saw the beauty of discipleship and the grace of God extended towards us in various seasons of our lives.

Growing up, she enjoyed exploring different creative mediums throughout her educational journey. But no matter the artistic outlet whether it be painting, drawing, or writing – the goal of using her gifts to help others has not changed. In college, she stumbled upon a field that would extend her love of design into a bigger context, and she got a bachelor's degree in Urban Design.

Truthfully speaking, being an author was not something that was on her radar. But this book, like much of her professional journey, is a testament to how God's plans for our life can surpass what we could imagine for ourselves. In elevating Christ, she hopes to encourage others to live surrendered to Jesus because if he can multiply 5 loaves and 2 fish –there is nothing that Our God cannot DO!

Petrice Dyer

Petrice Dyer is an Island girl from Jamaica. A mom of two beautiful girls, a mentor and an entrepreneur. She owns and operates Cradle by Jade Event Planning and Décor and is employed full-time. A purpose-driven woman blessed with innumerable talents. Recipient of the Esther Award "Business Category" for serving in the Women's Ministry in her local church.

Her guiding philosophy is "Whatever her mind perceives; she can achieve." One of her sole purposes in life is to help people in as many ways as she can. She is a catalyst for women supporting other women, and her dream is to see women being contagious with their talents and potential. She is a vibrant, inspirational speaker who confidently encourages people to rise above the difficulties they encounter.

Lacyann Nation

 Lacyann Nation is a native of Jamaica who moved to the United States at a very young age. She faced many struggles after losing her older sister, Teisha, in 2003. She cites God as being her strength and refuge through the years. She has now turned that loss into her fuel to continue pressing forward and making a difference in the lives of others.

Lacyann believes in being the light that shines through the darkness and illuminates all in its path with love and kindness. Lacyann has volunteered around her community with different organizations helping to bring awareness to sex trafficking, feeding the homeless, and supporting cancer survivors. She believes in always helping those in need and bringing awareness to those who suffer in silence.

She is a healthcare professional and an author who is passionate about what she does. She is a nurse in the intensive care unit and is currently working on her master's degree. She is a child of God and a wife who enjoys reading and spending quality time with her husband. Lacyann strives to be a blessing to others in whatever way God has blessed her.

Tecora Noble

Tecora Noble was born in Jamaica and lived most of her life in the United States. She's the mother of two amazing boys, Craig and Maison. Tecora enjoys singing and dancing and is actively involved in ministry, serving as a worship leader and prayer missionary for her local church. Tecora found and accepted Jesus in her late 20s, which she believes was the best decision she has ever made. She devotes her time to various organizations and associations, which sparked her interest in leadership, motivating her to complete her masters in Public Administration.

Tecora is a first-time author and gives all acknowledgement to the Holy Spirit for the inspirations of her sections. She lets her amusing personality sparkle through everything she does. Tecora has a very creative mindset and always tries to fashion opportunities that would benefit those around her and her community. She received the humanitarian award during her college tenure and still exudes the attributes of caring for those who are in need.

Tecora has a special interest in assisting widows, and hopes that one day she will be able to pursue a career involving the development of a program that will encourage and inspire hurting people. Tecora is a destiny helper who looks forward to the amazing path God has ordained for her.

Patrice Reid

 Patrice Reid aka The PR Networker is an Author, Host of The PUSH Talk Show, Speaker, Entrepreneur, Youth Pastor/Mentor and Founder of Push Youth Global Academy. She is also an ordained Minister & Evangelist with Christ for all Nations and holds a degree in Business Administration as well as Radio & Television Broadcasting.

Patrice is the visionary behind Daughters of the King (DOTK), a group that started on WhatsApp April 26th, 2016, with women from 4 continents around the world. The group offers words of encouragement and prayer for those who need a breakthrough and deliverance. In October 2019, she felt led to lead the women into 21 days of fasting and prayer, which at the end, resulted in the idea for this devotional book. Patrice is also the 2023 Presidential Lifetime Achievement Awards recipient, through the Christian Women in Leadership.

Patrice is called to connect people, especially women and youth on all levels, with the resources needed to Push them forward in life. She also believes we are more alike as women than we are different and should walk in unity for the purposes and Glory of God.

Currently, Patrice is pastoring and mentoring youth in her community and travels to preach the Gospel of Jesus to all nations. She also does a Global Prayer Conference with the DOTK group throughout the year.

Andre Weir–Leach

Andre Weir-Leach is an educator, motivational magnet and author of inspirational poems and stories. She is a Jamaican born who relocated to the North/ "Raptors" world with her husband and three wonderful kids. She enjoys photographing beautiful, picturesque views by the lake while on nature walks with her family on good days.

Andre's writing was developed after her conversion into God's kingdom. She wrote on a low scale before, but through the illumination of God's light, it quickly exploded, giving her insight into a talent God wanted her to purposefully use as a tool to win others for His kingdom.

Andre has a great passion for Christ, and a heart for people; especially women and youth. She combines these with her own journey of God's miraculous and life-changing power to counsel and encourage others. She has played many roles but, her greatest in which she is the least, is sharing God's liberating truth and wisdom to empower women and youth.

www.ingramcontent.com/pod-product-compliance
Lightning Source LLC
Chambersburg PA
CBHW071210120626
46546CB00006B/2493